Pam and the Clam

by Liza Charlesworth • illustrated by Doug Jones

SCHOLASTIC INC.

New York • Toronto • London • Auckland
Sydney • Mexico City • New Delhi • Hong Kong

Designed by Grafica, Inc.
ISBN: 978-0-545-68625-9
Copyright © 2009 by Lefty's Editorial Services.
All rights reserved. Published by Scholastic Inc.
SCHOLASTIC, LET'S LEARN READERS™, and associated logos are trademarks and/or registered trademarks of Scholastic Inc.

12 11 10 9 8 7 6 5 4 3 2 1   14 15 16 17 18 19/0

Printed in China.

The Am Family

What Is a Word Family?
A word family is a group of words that rhyme and share the same spelling pattern, such as *Pam*, *clam*, and *ram*. Read this story to learn more *-am* words!

This is **Pam**.
Pam is a member of the **Am** family.

One day, after she **swam**,
Pam saw a little **clam**.

And guess what?
That little **clam** talked!
He said, "I **am Sam** the amazing **clar**

Then **Sam** the **clam**
did some amazing things.

Sam rode a **ram**!

Sam juggled two apples and a **yam**!

Sam helped a beaver build a **dam**!

Sam painted a picture
with strawberry **jam**!

Sam told all the bullies to **scram**!

What else did **Sam** do?

Sam made a grand castle
just for **Pam**!

Yes, **Sam** could be a bit of a **ham**.
But he sure was an amazing **clam**!

Word Family House

Point to the *-am* word in each room and read it aloud.

ham | jam | yam
ram | slam | am
swam | Pam | scram
clam | | sham
cram | | scam

Word Family Match

Read each definition. Then go to the starfish and put your finger on the right -*am* word.

Definitions

1. a male sheep

2. a food like jelly

3. a sea creature with a shell

4. an orange vegetable

5. a girl's name

-am words

Word Family Maze

Help Pam find Sam. Put your finger on BEGIN. Then follow the trail of -*am* words to get to the END.

BEGIN

Pam	scram	spot
chin		
slam	yam	will
sham	am	
snack	mug	tack
ham	duck	
tin		
jam		
win	ram	
pack		
swam	chil
cram	bug	
Sam	clan

END